This Prayer Journal Belongs To

____

____

Hello God!
Its Me Again!

Today I Learned...

Today I'm Grateful For...

My Prayers Today...

Amen!

Hello God!
Its Me Again!

Today I Learned...

Today I'm Grateful For...

My Prayers Today...

Amen!

Hello God!
Its Me Again!

Today I Learned...

Today I'm Grateful For...

My Prayers Today...

Amen!

Hello God!
Its Me Again!

Today I Learned...

Today I'm Grateful For...

My Prayers Today...

Amen!

Hello God!
Its Me Again!

Today I Learned...

Today I'm Grateful For...

My Prayers Today...

Amen!

Hello God!
Its Me Again!

Today I Learned...

Today I'm Grateful For...

My Prayers Today...

Amen!

Hello God!
Its Me Again!

Today I Learned...

Today I'm Grateful For...

My Prayers Today...

Amen!

Hello God!
Its Me Again!

Today I Learned...

Today I'm Grateful For...

My Prayers Today...

Amen!

Hello God!
Its Me Again!

Today I Learned...

Today I'm Grateful For...

My Prayers Today...

Amen!

Hello God!
Its Me Again!

Today I Learned...

Today I'm Grateful For...

My Prayers Today...

Amen!

Hello God!
Its Me Again!

Today I Learned...

Today I'm Grateful For...

My Prayers Today...

Amen!

Hello God!
Its Me Again!

Today I Learned...

Today I'm Grateful For...

My Prayers Today...

Amen!

Hello God!
Its Me Again!

Today I Learned...

Today I'm Grateful For...

My Prayers Today...

Amen!

Hello God!
Its Me Again!

Today I Learned...

Today I'm Grateful For...

My Prayers Today...

Amen!

Hello God!
Its Me Again!

Today I Learned...

Today I'm Grateful For...

My Prayers Today...

Amen!

Hello God!
Its Me Again!

Today I Learned...

Today I'm Grateful For...

My Prayers Today...

Amen!

Hello God!
Its Me Again!

Today I Learned...

Today I'm Grateful For...

My Prayers Today...

Amen!

Hello God!
Its Me Again!

Today I Learned...

Today I'm Grateful For...

My Prayers Today...

Amen!

Hello God!
Its Me Again!

Today I Learned...

Today I'm Grateful For...

My Prayers Today...

Amen!

Hello God!
Its Me Again!

Today I Learned...

Today I'm Grateful For...

My Prayers Today...

Amen!

Hello God!
Its Me Again!

Today I Learned...

Today I'm Grateful For...

My Prayers Today...

Amen!

Hello God!
Its Me Again!

Today I Learned...

Today I'm Grateful For...

My Prayers Today...

Amen!

Hello God!
Its Me Again!

Today I Learned...

Today I'm Grateful For...

My Prayers Today...

Amen!

Hello God!
Its Me Again!

Today I Learned...

Today I'm Grateful For...

My Prayers Today...

Amen!

Hello God!
Its Me Again!

Today I Learned...

Today I'm Grateful For...

My Prayers Today...

Amen!

Hello God!
Its Me Again!

Today I Learned...

Today I'm Grateful For...

My Prayers Today...

Amen!

Hello God!
Its Me Again!

Today I Learned...

Today I'm Grateful For...

My Prayers Today...

Amen!

Hello God!
Its Me Again!

Today I Learned...

Today I'm Grateful For...

My Prayers Today...

Amen!

Hello God!
Its Me Again!

Today I Learned...

Today I'm Grateful For...

My Prayers Today...

Amen!

Hello God!
Its Me Again!

Today I Learned...

Today I'm Grateful For...

My Prayers Today...

Amen!

Hello God!
Its Me Again!

Today I Learned...

Today I'm Grateful For...

My Prayers Today...

Amen!

Hello God!
Its Me Again!

Today I Learned...

Today I'm Grateful For...

My Prayers Today...

Amen!

Hello God!
Its Me Again!

Today I Learned...

Today I'm Grateful For...

My Prayers Today...

Amen!

Hello God!
Its Me Again!

Today I Learned...

Today I'm Grateful For...

My Prayers Today...

Amen!

Hello God!
Its Me Again!

Today I Learned...

Today I'm Grateful For...

My Prayers Today...

Amen!

Hello God!
Its Me Again!

Today I Learned...

Today I'm Grateful For...

My Prayers Today...

Amen!

Hello God!
Its Me Again!

Today I Learned...

Today I'm Grateful For...

My Prayers Today...

Amen!

Hello God!
Its Me Again!

Today I Learned...

Today I'm Grateful For...

My Prayers Today...

Amen!

Hello God!
Its Me Again!

Today I Learned...

Today I'm Grateful For...

My Prayers Today...

Amen!

Hello God!
Its Me Again!

Today I Learned...

Today I'm Grateful For...

My Prayers Today...

Amen!

Hello God!
Its Me Again!

Today I Learned...

Today I'm Grateful For...

My Prayers Today...

Amen!

Hello God!
Its Me Again!

Today I Learned...

Today I'm Grateful For...

My Prayers Today...

Amen!

Hello God!
Its Me Again!

Today I Learned...

Today I'm Grateful For...

My Prayers Today...

Amen!

Hello God!
Its Me Again!

Today I Learned...

Today I'm Grateful For...

My Prayers Today...

Amen!

Hello God!
Its Me Again!

Today I Learned...

Today I'm Grateful For...

My Prayers Today...

Amen!

Hello God!
Its Me Again!

Today I Learned...

Today I'm Grateful For...

My Prayers Today...

Amen!

Hello God!
Its Me Again!

Today I Learned...

Today I'm Grateful For...

My Prayers Today...

Amen!

Hello God!
Its Me Again!

Today I Learned...

Today I'm Grateful For...

My Prayers Today...

Amen!

Hello God!
Its Me Again!

Today I Learned...

Today I'm Grateful For...

My Prayers Today...

Amen!

Hello God!
Its Me Again!

Today I Learned...

Today I'm Grateful For...

My Prayers Today...

Amen!

Hello God!
Its Me Again!

Today I Learned...

Today I'm Grateful For...

My Prayers Today...

Amen!

Hello God!
Its Me Again!

Today I Learned...

Today I'm Grateful For...

My Prayers Today...

Amen!

Hello God!
Its Me Again!

Today I Learned...

Today I'm Grateful For...

My Prayers Today...

Amen!

Hello God!
Its Me Again!

Today I Learned...

Today I'm Grateful For...

My Prayers Today...

Amen!

Hello God!
Its Me Again!

Today I Learned...

Today I'm Grateful For...

My Prayers Today...

Amen!

Hello God!
Its Me Again!

Today I Learned...

Today I'm Grateful For...

My Prayers Today...

Amen!

Hello God!
Its Me Again!

Today I Learned...

Today I'm Grateful For...

My Prayers Today...

Amen!

Hello God!
Its Me Again!

Today I Learned...

Today I'm Grateful For...

My Prayers Today...

Amen!

Hello God!
Its Me Again!

Today I Learned...

Today I'm Grateful For...

My Prayers Today...

Amen!

Hello God!
Its Me Again!

Today I Learned...

Today I'm Grateful For...

My Prayers Today...

Amen!

Hello God!
Its Me Again!

Today I Learned...

Today I'm Grateful For...

My Prayers Today...

Amen!

Hello God!
Its Me Again!

Today I Learned...

Today I'm Grateful For...

My Prayers Today...

Amen!

Hello God!
Its Me Again!

Today I Learned...

Today I'm Grateful For...

My Prayers Today...

Amen!

Hello God!
Its Me Again!

Today I Learned...

Today I'm Grateful For...

My Prayers Today...

Amen!

Hello God!
Its Me Again!

Today I Learned...

Today I'm Grateful For...

My Prayers Today...

Amen!

Hello God!
Its Me Again!

Today I Learned...

Today I'm Grateful For...

My Prayers Today...

Amen!

Hello God!
Its Me Again!

Today I Learned...

Today I'm Grateful For...

My Prayers Today...

Amen!

Hello God!
Its Me Again!

Today I Learned...

Today I'm Grateful For...

My Prayers Today...

Amen!

Hello God!
Its Me Again!

Today I Learned...

Today I'm Grateful For...

My Prayers Today...

Amen!

Hello God!
Its Me Again!

Today I Learned...

Today I'm Grateful For...

My Prayers Today...

Amen!

Hello God!
Its Me Again!

Today I Learned...

Today I'm Grateful For...

My Prayers Today...

Amen!

Hello God!
Its Me Again!

Today I Learned...

Today I'm Grateful For...

My Prayers Today...

Amen!

Hello God!
Its Me Again!

Today I Learned...

Today I'm Grateful For...

My Prayers Today...

Amen!

Hello God!
Its Me Again!

Today I Learned...

Today I'm Grateful For...

My Prayers Today...

Amen!

Hello God!
Its Me Again!

Today I Learned...

Today I'm Grateful For...

My Prayers Today...

Amen!

Hello God!
Its Me Again!

Today I Learned...

Today I'm Grateful For...

My Prayers Today...

Amen!

Hello God!
Its Me Again!

Today I Learned...

Today I'm Grateful For...

My Prayers Today...

Amen!

Hello God!
Its Me Again!

Today I Learned...

Today I'm Grateful For...

My Prayers Today...

Amen!

Hello God!
Its Me Again!

Today I Learned...

Today I'm Grateful For...

My Prayers Today...

Amen!

Hello God!
Its Me Again!

Today I Learned...

Today I'm Grateful For...

My Prayers Today...

Amen!

Hello God!
Its Me Again!

Today I Learned...

Today I'm Grateful For...

My Prayers Today...

Amen!

Hello God!
Its Me Again!

Today I Learned...

Today I'm Grateful For...

My Prayers Today...

Amen!

Hello God!
Its Me Again!

Today I Learned...

Today I'm Grateful For...

My Prayers Today...

Amen!

Hello God!
Its Me Again!

Today I Learned...

Today I'm Grateful For...

My Prayers Today...

Amen!

Hello God!
Its Me Again!

Today I Learned...

Today I'm Grateful For...

My Prayers Today...

Amen!

Hello God!
Its Me Again!

Today I Learned...

Today I'm Grateful For...

My Prayers Today...

Amen!

Hello God!
Its Me Again!

Today I Learned...

Today I'm Grateful For...

My Prayers Today...

Amen!

Hello God!
Its Me Again!

Today I Learned...

Today I'm Grateful For...

My Prayers Today...

Amen!

Hello God!
Its Me Again!

Today I Learned...

Today I'm Grateful For...

My Prayers Today...

Amen!

Hello God!
Its Me Again!

Today I Learned...

Today I'm Grateful For...

My Prayers Today...

Amen!

Hello God!
Its Me Again!

Today I Learned...

Today I'm Grateful For...

My Prayers Today...

Amen!

Hello God!
Its Me Again!

Today I Learned...

Today I'm Grateful For...

My Prayers Today...

Amen!

Hello God!
Its Me Again!

Today I Learned...

Today I'm Grateful For...

My Prayers Today...

Amen!

Hello God!
Its Me Again!

Today I Learned...

Today I'm Grateful For...

My Prayers Today...

Amen!

Hello God!
Its Me Again!

Today I Learned...

Today I'm Grateful For...

My Prayers Today...

Amen!

Hello God!
Its Me Again!

Today I Learned...

Today I'm Grateful For...

My Prayers Today...

Amen!

Hello God!
Its Me Again!

Today I Learned...

Today I'm Grateful For...

My Prayers Today...

Amen!

Hello God!
Its Me Again!

Today I Learned...

Today I'm Grateful For...

My Prayers Today...

Amen!

Hello God!
Its Me Again!

Today I Learned...

Today I'm Grateful For...

My Prayers Today...

Amen!

Hello God!
Its Me Again!

Today I Learned...

Today I'm Grateful For...

My Prayers Today...

Amen

88126161R00057